Brown Angels

WALTER DEAN MYERS

Brown Angels

AN ALBUM OF PICTURES AND VERSE

HarperCollins*Publishers*

J Kaiell
1996

ALSO BY WALTER DEAN MYERS

Scorpions

The Mouse Rap

Now Is Your Time!
The African-American Struggle for Freedom

The Righteous Revenge
of Artemis Bonner

Photographs on pages 8 and 16 used by permission of
the Library of Congress. Photographs on pages 12, 22, 31, 37 (girl on
bicycle and baby in basin), and 39 used by courtesy of the Richard Samuel
Roberts Estate. Photograph on page 25 used by permission of the Oregon
Historical Society. Remaining photographs are
from the author's collection.

Brown Angels
An Album of Pictures and Verse
Copyright © 1993 by Walter Dean Myers
Printed in the U.S.A. All rights reserved.

Library of Congress Cataloging-in-Publication Data
Myers, Walter Dean, date
  Brown angels : an album of pictures and verse / by Walter Dean
Myers.
    p.   cm.
  Summary: A collection of poems, accompanied by photographs, about
African American children living around the turn of the century.
  ISBN 0-06-022917-9. — ISBN 0-06-022918-7 (lib. bdg.)
  1. Afro-Americans—Juvenile poetry.   2. Children's poetry, American.
[1. Afro-Americans—Poetry.   2. American poetry.]   I. Title.
PS3563.Y48B76   1993   92-36792
811'.54—dc20   CIP
                                                                     AC

5   6   7   8   9   10
❖

Brown Angels

hy do I love children? I think it is because the child in each of us is our most precious part. Children remind us of a time of innocence, a time of giving, and an unfettered love of life.

Combing through dusty bins in antique shops, flea markets, auction houses, and museum collections to find these pictures of African-American children was a sheer delight. Seeing their faces scrubbed and beaming, seeing them dressed in their Sunday best for a traveling photographer, told me what our grandparents and great-grandparents thought of their children. These pictures speak to me of hardworking people—of tenant farmers, porters, and teachers of the "colored" schools—who celebrated the lives of their babies as have all people before them and since. And they did so despite the difficulties of their own lives.

First there were ten pictures that I cherished, then a hundred, then several hundred carefully tucked away in my files. I cherish the chance to publish these pictures. I cherish the chance to share the pride of the parents and guardians who dressed them for the sitting. I cherish the chance to share the sensitivity of the photographers to their beauty. The poems were inspired sometimes by the pictures, sometimes by the memory of children I have known, and sometimes just by the joy of a summer day.

I hope that these pictures bring you as much happiness as they have brought me. Perhaps they will send you to mothers, aunts, grandmothers, and great-grandmothers to search for pictures and memories of your own.

Walter Dean Myers

Friendship

There is a secret thread that makes us friends
          Turn away from hard and breakful eyes
          Turn away from cold and painful lies
That speaks of other, more important ends
There are two hard yet tender hearts that beat
          Take always my hand at special times
          Take always my dark and precious rhymes
That sing so brightly when our glad souls meet

Blossoms

I never dreamt
that tender blossoms
would be brown
Or precious angels
could come down
to live in the garden
of my giving heart
But here you are
brown angel

Love That Boy

Love that boy,
like a rabbit loves to run
I said I love that boy
like a rabbit loves to run
Love to call him in the morning
love to call him
"Hey there, son!"

He walk like his grandpa
grins like his uncle Ben
I said he walk like his grandpa
and grins like his uncle Ben
Grins when he happy
when he sad he grins again

His mama like to hold him
like to feed him cherry pie
I said his mama like to hold him
feed him that cherry pie
She can have him now
I'll get him by and by

He got long roads to walk down,
before the setting sun
I said he got a long, long road
to walk down,
before the setting sun
He'll be a long stride walker
and a good man before he done

Zudie O, Zudie O

Zudie O, Zudie O
Chug on down
Swing your hips
All round the town
Zudie O, Zudie O
What you see?
Fine black boys
From Sangaree
Zudie O, Zudie O
Where you been?
Akuba-Lan
And back again
Zudie O, Zudie O
Where you going?
Anywhere
The Wind is blowing

Prayer

Shout my name to the angels
Sing my song to the skies
Anoint my ears with wisdom
Let beauty fill my eyes

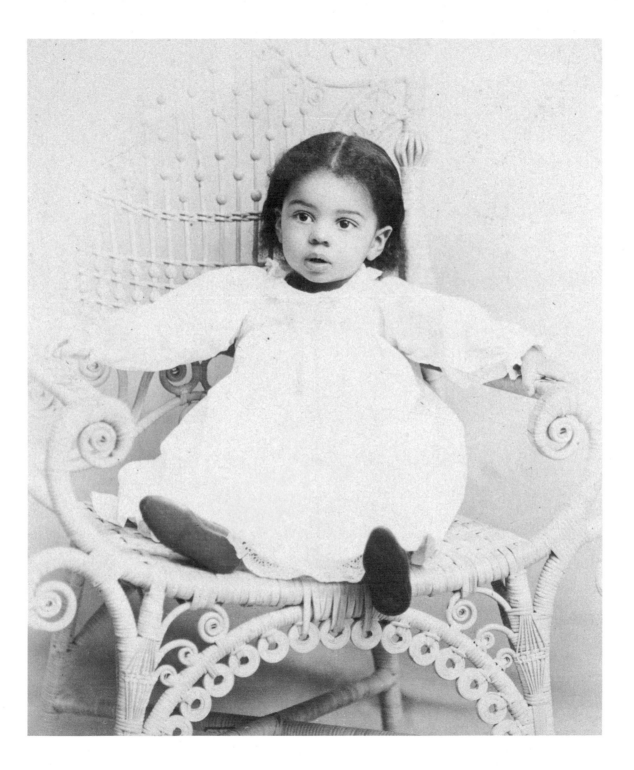

For I am dark and precious
And have such gifts to give
Sweet joy, sweet love,
Sweet laughter
Sweet wondrous life to live

Pierson Brothers   Elizabeth, N. J.
                          Nanepashemet, Mass.

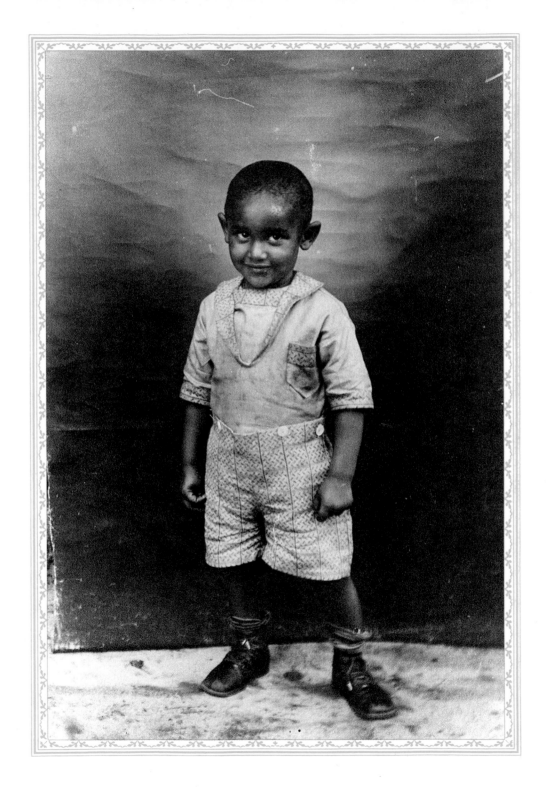

They

They say you don't know a blessed thing
Ain't that something?
Say you just smiling cause
You don't have nothing else to do
You ever hear of such a thing?

I think it's them old folks
Who don't know nothing
Them with their old serious selves
A-scuffling and a-snuffling
And being so tizzy-busy
They don't remember
How good a grin feels
Ain't that something
How people forget that?
Ain't you surprised?
I thought you would be!

Jolly, Jolly

Jolly, Jolly, sweet and brown
Jolly, Jolly, gee
Jolly is the lucky child
Who looks like me!

Summary

I like hot days, hot days
Sweat is what you got days
Bugs buzzin from cousin to cousin
Juices dripping
Running and ripping
Catch the one you love days

Birds peeping
Old men sleeping
Lazy days, daisies lay
Beaming and dreaming
Of hot days, hot days,
Sweat is what you got days

Pretty Little Black Girl

Pretty little black girl
Sweet as you can be
Wiggle waggle, wiggle waggle
One, two, three

Pretty little tan girl

She knows all the tricks

Wiggle waggle, wiggle waggle

Four, five, six

Pretty little brown girl
You know you sing so fine
Wiggle waggle, wiggle waggle
Seven, eight, nine

Pretty little coffee girl
She knows how to win
Wiggle waggle, wiggle waggle
We've reached ten!

Grey,

2140 THIRD AVENUE,
BET. 116TH & 117TH STREETS, N. Y.

Jeannie Had a Giggle

Jeannie had a giggle just beneath her toes
She gave a little wiggle and up her leg it rose

She tried to grab the giggle as it shimmied past her knees
But it slid right past her fingers with a "'scuse me if you please"

It slipped around her middle, it made her jump and shout
Jeannie wanted that giggle in, that giggle wanted out!

Jeannie closed her mouth, but then she heard a funny sound
As out that silly giggle flew and jumped down to the ground

Jeannie caught it with her foot just beneath her toes
She gave a little wiggle and up her leg it rose

Pride

The sound of their steps
has long been gone
Black foot, strong foot,
stumbling on
Oh follow the memory!

The sound of their song

has long been gone

Black song, strong song,

souls singing on

Oh cherish the memory!

The depth of their pride

will never be gone

Black hearts, strong hearts,

hearts beating on

Oh honor the memory!